Can You Find It?
AMERICA

Can You Find It?
AMERICA

Linda Falken

The Metropolitan Museum of Art

Abrams Books for Young Readers

New York

In this print of
the western frontier,
can you find

1

bell

2

boats

2

women holding children

1

ladder

5

horses

2

axes

6

covered wagons

2

tents

When you look at a work of art, you first see the image as a whole. But many works are filled with intriguing details—and it can be great fun to search and discover these hidden treasures.

In the first *Can You Find It?* book, we featured paintings from the collection of The Metropolitan Museum of Art. In *Can You Find It, Too?*, we also included paintings from three other American museums and museums in London, Paris, Vienna, Florence, and Madrid. Now, in *Can You Find It? America*, we've returned to the collection of the Metropolitan Museum. This time, you'll find images of prints and textiles as well as of paintings. From an eighteenth-century needlework landscape to a late-twentieth-century painting of a chance encounter between two artists, each work is characteristically American and each is filled with a wealth of details for you to discover.

You can also play the "Can You Find It?" game whenever you visit a museum with a companion. Take turns finding some details that you can count in a work of art and challenging each other to find them. You'll discover that the more you look, the more you find—and you'll never look at art the same way again.

—Linda Falken

In this painting of
a plantation,
can you find

1

millwheel

1

weeping willow

2

weather vanes

7

bunches of grapes

1

man fishing

3

large birds

4

smoking chimneys

1

American flag

The Plantation (detail)
American, ca. 1825
Oil on wood

In this painting of
George Washington,
can you find

4

fur hats

1

bandage

3

horses

1

spur

2

ponytails

2

fringed scarves

3

tassels

1

gold earring

In this painting of
a cider mill,
can you find

1

hat with a feather

2

Canada geese

1

broken arm

1

shovel

2

bare feet

1

fish

1

man reading a newspaper

&

the date 1840

Cider Making (detail)
William Sidney Mount, American, 1807–1868
Oil on canvas, 1840–41

In this embroidery of
a countryside,
can you find

2

windmills

1

dog

2

sickles

7

large birds

1

picnic basket

2

squirrels

3

butterflies

1

snail

Embroidered Chair Back
Mehitable Starkey, American, b. 1739
Wool and silk on linen, ca. 1755–65

In this painting of
John Brown,
can you find

5

children

2

feathers

4

red stripes

1

armband

21

gold buttons

1

sheet of paper

1

green kerchief

&

the initials JG

The Last Moments of John Brown (detail)
Thomas Hovenden, American
(b. in Ireland), 1840–1895
Oil on canvas, 1882–84

In this painting of
a railroad depot,
can you find

1

hot-air balloon

2

men on rooftops

1

woman selling produce

3

American flags

1

horse rearing

1

child waving

1

clock

&

a man standing on one foot

The Third Avenue Railroad Depot (detail)
William H. Schenck, American, active ca. 1854–1864
Oil on canvas, ca. 1859–60

In this painting of
**a Native American
encampment,**
can you find

5

dogs

1

campfire

3

waterfalls

1

horse grazing

5

tepees

1

colt

1

stag

1

skull

The Rocky Mountains, Lander's Peak (detail)
Albert Bierstadt, American (b. in Germany), 1830–1902
Oil on canvas, 1863

In this print of
a steamboat race,
can you find

2

American flags

6

men waving hats

1

flatboat

1

pair of antlers

11

smokestacks

2

staircases

1

ladder

&

the letter N, backward

The Champions of the Mississippi. "A Race for the Buckhorns." (detail)
Frances Flora Bond Palmer, American (b. in England), 1812–1876, artist;
Currier & Ives, American, active 1852–1907, publisher
Hand-colored lithograph, 1866

In this print of
a blacksmith's forge,
can you find

2

bellows

3

white horses

1

striped shirt

2

pairs of tongs

2

barrels

27

horseshoes

1

clock

1

cane

"Trotting Cracks" at the Forge. (detail)
Currier & Ives, American, active 1852–1907, publisher
Hand-colored lithograph, 1868

In this painting of
a church,
can you find

4

dogs

1

open window

2

produce stands

3

streetlights

1

boy running

1

rooster

2

green shutters

3

flags

**The North Dutch Church, Fulton
and William Streets, New York**
Edward Lamson Henry,
American, 1841–1919
Oil on academy board, 1869

22

In this detail of
a crazy quilt,
can you find

1

blue bow

2

spiders

1

large butterfly

1

bride and groom

4

feathers

1

fairy

3

sets of interlocking rings

1

crescent

Quilt (detail)
Elizabeth Hickock Keeler, American, 1847–1926;
Ellie Keeler Gorham, American, 1873–1965
Silk, silk velvet, silk thread, metallic beads,
and ink, ca. 1883

In this painting of
farmland,
can you find

1

pipe

1

dog

2

cows

5

men at work

1

straw hat

1

porch

4

tall haystacks

1

silo

Janitor's Holiday (detail)
Paul Sample, American, 1896–1974
Oil on canvas, 1936

25

In this print of the
American Wing
of The Metropolitan
Museum of Art,
can you find

1

bird

8

top hats

1

cat

3

parasols

5

walking sticks

1

barrel

1

dog

1

pair of glasses

In this painting of New York City's **Wall Street,** can you find

1

Statue of Liberty

3

horns

1

clock

4

drumsticks

1

red sash

1

streetlight

2

bouquets of flowers

&

the abbreviation US twice

The Cathedrals of Wall Street
Florine Stettheimer,
American, 1871–1944
Oil on canvas, 1939

27

In this painting of
a city street,
can you find

1

chain

1

briefcase

1

fire hydrant

2

pairs of suspenders

1

flag

1

blue hat

6

wheels

1

child

The Photographer (detail)
Jacob Lawrence, American, 1917–2000
Watercolor, gouache, and pencil on paper, 1942

In this painting of
a farmyard,
can you find

1

dog

7

turkeys

1

tree stump

2

chimneys

1

circular saw

1

boy running

4

gray-haired people

&

the name Moses

Thanksgiving Turkey (detail)
Anna Mary Robertson Moses, American, 1860–1961
Oil on wood, 1943

In this painting of
two artists,
can you find

1

saxophone

4

taxicabs

1

palette

4

swords

3

traffic lights

1

police officer

1

apple core

&

the date 1807

Chance Encounter at 3 A.M. (detail)
Red Grooms, American, b. 1937
Oil on canvas, 1984

32

In this painted quilt of

an apartment building,

can you find

3

wrecked cars

1

raised fist

9

gray-haired people

1

purse

1

person peering through blinds

5

fire hoses

2

window guards

&

the number 222 three times

Street Story Quilt (detail)
Faith Ringgold, American, b. 1930
Oil, ink marker, dyed fabric, and sequins on canvas,
sewn to quilted fabric, 1985

the western frontier, pages 2–3

- 1 bell
- 2 boats
- 2 women holding children
- 1 ladder
- 5 horses
- 2 axes
- 6 covered wagons
- 2 tents

Across the Continent. "Westward the Course of Empire Takes Its Way." (detail)
Frances Flora Bond Palmer, artist; James Merritt Ives, lithographer;
Currier & Ives, publisher

Between 1835 and 1907, the firm of N. Currier, later Currier & Ives, created lithographic prints on more than 4,000 subjects. Longtime staff artist Frances "Franny" Palmer drew scores of pictures, often creating the color models as well. In this 1868 print celebrating the country's westward movement, a railroad divides civilization in the form of a frontier town from the natural world of Native Americans. The train represents the transcontinental railroad, which would be completed the following year.

17¾ x 27¼ in.
Gift of George S. Amory, in memory of his wife, Renée Carhart Amory, 1966   66.738.23

a plantation, pages 6–7

- 1 millwheel
- 1 weeping willow
- 2 weather vanes
- 7 bunches of grapes
- 1 man fishing
- 3 large birds
- 4 smoking chimneys
- 1 American flag

The Plantation (detail), American

This painting by an unknown American folk artist pictures a plantation, but in a more decorative than realistic manner. The graceful branches of the trees, leaves fluttering in the breeze, waves rolling down the river, and curving paths all provide a sense of rhythm and movement, while the placement of the two large trees, the houses, and the ship provide balance and a sense of symmetry.

19⅛ x 29½ in.
Gift of Edgar William and Bernice Chrysler Garbisch, 1963   63.201.3

George Washington, pages 8–9

- 4 fur hats
- 1 bandage
- 3 horses
- 1 spur
- 2 ponytails
- 2 fringed scarves
- 3 tassels
- 1 gold earring

Washington Crossing the Delaware (detail), Emanuel Leutze

Emanuel Leutze based this huge painting on a real event that changed the course of the American Revolution. After the colonists had lost several battles, support for the war was down. Then, on a stormy Christmas night in 1776, George Washington led about 2,400 troops across the icy Delaware River to launch a surprise attack on British troops in Trenton, New Jersey. Washington won the battle, and the victory boosted the colonists' morale, inspiring them to keep fighting for independence and democracy.

12 ft. 5 in. x 21 ft. 3 in.
Gift of John Stewart Kennedy, 1897   97.34

a cider mill, pages 10–11

- 1 hat with a feather
- 2 Canada geese
- 1 broken arm
- 1 shovel
- 2 bare feet
- 1 fish
- 1 man reading a newspaper
- & the date 1840

Cider Making (detail), William Sidney Mount

Though William Sidney Mount accurately pictured cider making at a real mill in Setauket, New York, his painting also referred to political events of the time. William Henry Harrison ran for president as a "man of the people" who preferred a log cabin and hard cider to the fancy tastes of his opponent, Martin Van Buren. Harrison won the election, but died of pneumonia just one month after making an hour-and-forty-five-minute-long inauguration speech on the steps of the White House during a snowstorm.

27 x 34⅛ in.
Purchase, Bequest of Charles Allen Munn, by exchange, 1966   66.126

a countryside, page 12

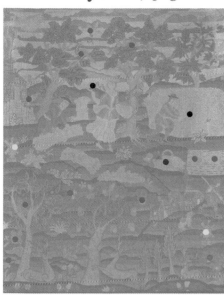

- 2 windmills
- 1 dog
- 2 sickles
- 7 large birds
- 1 picnic basket
- 2 squirrels
- 3 butterflies
- 1 snail

Embroidered Chair Back
Mehitable Starkey

This needlework panel was made in the mid-1700s by Mehitable Starkey and passed down in her family until the late twentieth century. Though most Boston needlework pictures were horizontal in composition, Starkey's is vertical. It's thought that the picture was meant to cover the back panel of an easy chair, such as the Museum's Newport easy chair from the same time period, which features a needlework landscape of similar size on the back panel.

35 x 25 in.
Gift of Philip Holzer, 2003   2003.480

John Brown, page 13

- 5 children
- 2 feathers
- 4 red stripes
- 1 armband
- 21 gold buttons
- 1 sheet of paper
- 1 green kerchief
- & the initials JG

The Last Moments of John Brown
(detail), Thomas Hovenden

In 1859, John Brown led a raid on the federal arsenal in Harper's Ferry, West Virginia, intending to arm slaves for a revolt. The attack failed, and Brown was captured, tried, and sentenced to hang. Thomas Hovenden later based his painting on an account of Brown being led to the gallows that had appeared in the *New York Tribune* shortly after he was hanged. The article was inaccurate—the public was not, in fact, allowed near Brown—but whether Hovenden was aware of that is not known.

77⅜ x 66¼ in.
Gift of Mr. and Mrs. Carl Stoeckel, 1897   97.5

a railroad depot, pages 14–15

- 1 hot-air balloon
- 2 men on rooftops
- 1 woman selling produce
- 3 American flags
- 1 horse rearing
- 1 child waving
- 1 clock
- & a man standing on one foot

The Third Avenue Railroad Depot (detail), William H. Schenck

William H. Schenck was superintendent of the Third Avenue Railroad when he painted this trolley turnaround. At the time, the depot stood on Third Avenue between 65th and 66th Streets in New York City. On June 27, 1861, just a year after Schenck finished his painting, the depot was destroyed in a fire. Today, the site is occupied by Manhattan House, an apartment building in the Modernist style.

36 x 50 in.
The Edward W. C. Arnold Collection of New York Prints, Maps, and Pictures,
Bequest of Edward W. C. Arnold, 1954   54.90.178

a Native American encampment, pages 16–17

- 5 dogs
- 1 campfire
- 3 waterfalls
- 1 horse grazing
- 5 tepees
- 1 colt
- 1 stag
- 1 skull

The Rocky Mountains, Lander's Peak (detail), Albert Bierstadt

In 1859, Albert Bierstadt accompanied a government survey expedition led by Colonel Frederick W. Lander to the Nebraska Territory. The painting, made from sketches after his return to the East, pictures a tribe of Shoshone camped beside the Green River at the base of the Wind River Range in what is now Wyoming. Following Colonel Lander's death in the Civil War, Bierstadt named the central mountain in the painting Lander's Peak.

73½ in. x 10 ft. ¾ in.
Rogers Fund, 1907   07.123

a steamboat race, pages 18–19

- 2 American flags
- 6 men waving hats
- 1 flatboat
- 1 pair of antlers
- 11 smokestacks
- 2 staircases
- 1 ladder
- & the letter N, backward

The Champions of the Mississippi. "A Race for the Buckhorns." (detail)
Frances Flora Bond Palmer, artist; Currier & Ives, publisher

John Fitch designed and launched the first American steamboat in 1787 but failed to make a commercial success of it, as Robert Fulton would do twenty years later. On the Mississippi River, paddlewheel steamboats came to dominate both passenger and freight trade for most of the 1800s, and steamboat races were popular. In the race shown, the buckhorns—or antlers—were the prize, and whichever boat won would get to mount them high between its smokestacks for the next year.

18⅜ x 27¾ in.
Bequest of Adele S. Colgate, 1962   63.550.42

a blacksmith's forge, pages 20–21

- 2 bellows
- 3 white horses
- 1 striped shirt
- 2 pairs of tongs
- 2 barrels
- 27 horseshoes
- 1 clock
- 1 cane

"Trotting Cracks" at the Forge. (detail), Currier & Ives, publisher

"Trotting cracks" is a nineteenth-century slang term for fast horses. Though artist Thomas Worth (American, 1834–1917) was not on the staff of Currier & Ives, he contributed greatly to the firm's success. One of his drawings was the basis for this lithograph of a busy blacksmith's forge. Inside are shown three well-known trotters of the time—from front to back, Lady Thorn, Grey Eagle, and Mountain Boy.

19¼ x 29¼ in.
Bequest of Adele S. Colgate, 1962   63.550.277

a church, page 22

- 4 dogs
- 1 open window
- 2 produce stands
- 3 streetlights
- 1 boy running
- 1 rooster
- 2 green shutters
- 3 flags

The North Dutch Church, Fulton and William Streets, New York
Edward Lamson Henry

During the Revolutionary War, the British gutted the North Dutch Church, shipping its beautiful pulpit to England and using its pews and woodwork for fuel. The building was then used for storage, as a hospital, and as a prison before being restored and reopened as a church after the war. Edward Lamson Henry painted the church in 1869, one hundred years after it was built. That same year, the land it stood on was sold, and in 1875, the church was demolished.

18 x 14 in.
Bequest of Maria DeWitt Jesup, from the collection of her husband, Morris K. Jesup, 1914   15.30.66

a crazy quilt, page 23

- 1 blue bow
- 2 spiders
- 1 large butterfly
- 1 bride and groom
- 4 feathers
- 1 fairy
- 3 sets of interlocking rings
- 1 crescent

Quilt (detail), Elizabeth Hickock Keeler and Ellie Keeler Gorham

In the late 1800s, crazy quilts were so popular that manufacturers offered ready-to-sew kits with pre-cut fabric and instructions on how to piece the blocks together. Filled with brightly colored fabric and patches with hand-drawn figures, this quilt also includes a commercially made patch of silk showing a fairy and a wreath of flowers. A mother-daughter project, the quilt was made when Ellie Keeler was about ten years old.

74¾ x 68¼ in.
Gift of the Gorham and Nancarrow families, 1993   1993.101

farmland, pages 24–25

- 1 pipe
- 1 dog
- 2 cows
- 5 men at work
- 1 straw hat
- 1 porch
- 4 tall haystacks
- 1 silo

Janitor's Holiday (detail), Paul Sample

Shortly after graduating from college with a degree in architecture, Paul Sample contracted tuberculosis. While being treated, he met the artist Jonas Lie and took up painting. After he recovered, Sample decided to study art. In the early 1930s, he worked in the Social Realist style, picturing urban workers who were affected by the Great Depression. He then shifted to Regionalism, painting agricultural workers in rural landscapes such as that shown in *Janitor's Holiday*.

26 x 40 in.
Arthur Hoppock Hearn Fund, 1937   37.60.1

Wall Street, page 27

- 1 Statue of Liberty
- 3 horns
- 1 clock
- 4 drumsticks
- 1 red sash
- 1 streetlight
- 2 bouquets of flowers
- & the abbreviation US twice

The Cathedrals of Wall Street
Florine Stettheimer

Between 1929 and 1944, Florine Stettheimer painted a series of four "Cathedral" pictures that cleverly commented on the fast-paced life of New York City. In this 1939 painting, a band parades down Wall Street in the city's financial district, where 150 years earlier, George Washington was inaugurated as president of the United States.

60 x 50 in.
Gift of Ettie Stettheimer, 1953   53.24.2

American Wing, page 26

- 1 bird
- 8 top hats
- 1 cat
- 3 parasols
- 5 walking sticks
- 1 barrel
- 1 dog
- 1 pair of glasses

***American Wing of
The Metropolitan Museum of Art***
(detail), Thomas Maitland Cleland

Born in Brooklyn, New York, Thomas Maitland Cleland became a painter, typographer, and printer. He painted this poster as an advertisement for the American Wing at The Metropolitan Museum of Art, which opened to the public in 1924. The American Wing was the first permanent installation in an art museum of American colonial and early federal decorative arts and architecture.

42½ x 30¾ in.
The Metropolitan Museum of Art

a city street, pages 28–29

- 1 chain
- 1 briefcase
- 1 fire hydrant
- 2 pairs of suspenders
- 1 flag
- 1 blue hat
- 6 wheels
- 1 child

The Photographer (detail), Jacob Lawrence

In 1942, after creating several series depicting African American history, Jacob Lawrence turned to the daily life of Harlem, New York, the community in which he lived. Working with watercolor, gouache, and pencil—some of the same materials he was introduced to as a young boy—he created a series of thirty paintings, including *The Photographer*, which shows a well-dressed family having its picture taken in the midst of a bustling street scene.

22⅛ x 30½ in.
Purchase, Lila Acheson Wallace Gift, 2001   2001.205

a farmyard, pages 30–31

- 1 dog
- 7 turkeys
- 1 tree stump
- 2 chimneys
- 1 circular saw
- 1 boy running
- 4 gray-haired people
- & the name Moses

Thanksgiving Turkey (detail), Anna Mary Robertson Moses

After thirty years of campaigning for Thanksgiving to become a national holiday, Sara Josepha Hale, editor of *Godey's Lady's Book* and author of "Mary Had a Little Lamb," got her wish. In 1863, President Abraham Lincoln proclaimed the fourth Thursday in November as Thanksgiving Day. Here, self-taught artist Anna Mary Robertson Moses, better known as Grandma Moses, painted a family catching the Thanksgiving turkey. Though Moses did not begin painting seriously until she was in her seventies, she created more than 1,500 paintings before her death at age 101.

15⅛ x 19⅛ in.
Bequest of Mary Stillman Harkness, 1950   50.145.375

two artists, pages 32–33

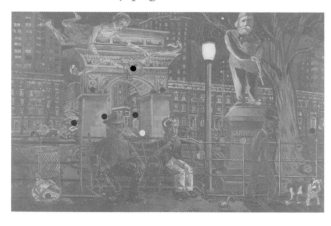

- 1 saxophone
- 4 taxicabs
- 1 palette
- 4 swords
- 3 traffic lights
- 1 police officer
- 1 apple core
- & the date 1807

Chance Encounter at 3 A.M. (detail), Red Grooms

Red Grooms got the idea for his painting from an article he read in *The New York Times Magazine* (November 20, 1983), which recounted how early one morning Willem de Kooning (American, b. in Netherlands, 1904–1997, right) and Mark Rothko (American, b. in Russia, 1903–1970, left) met by chance when they happened to sit on the same bench in New York City's Washington Square Park. Grooms imagined the two artists eyeing each other moments before introducing themselves, while overhead hovers a muse holding an artist's palette and brushes.

8 ft. 4 in. x 12 ft. 11 in.
Purchase, Mr. and Mrs. Wolfgang Schoenborn Gift, 1984   1984.194

an apartment building, pages 34–35

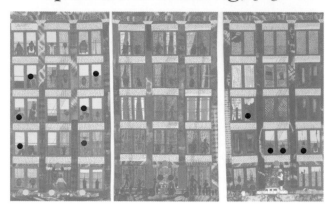

- 3 wrecked cars
- 1 raised fist
- 9 gray-haired people
- 1 purse
- 1 person peering through blinds
- 5 fire hoses
- 2 window guards
- & the number 222 three times

Street Story Quilt (detail), Faith Ringgold

In her painted quilts, Faith Ringgold combines images and handwritten text to explore race and feminism through characters that serve as urban American folk heroes. Here, she tells the story of A. J., who is raised by his grandmother after losing his mother and brothers in a car accident and his father in a fire. Though A. J. can't seem to stay out of trouble, he holds on to his dream of becoming an author. After years of struggle, he succeeds and returns in a limousine to take his grandmother back to California with him.

90 in. x 12 ft.
Arthur Hoppock Hearn Fund and funds from various donors, 1990   1990.237a–c

a snowy street, back cover

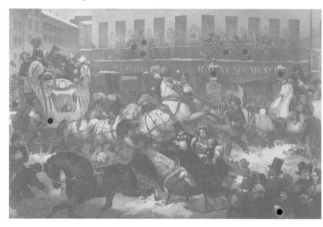

- 2 stars
- 1 giraffe
- 1 newspaper
- 2 streetlamps
- 1 winged horse
- 2 drums
- 6 fur muffs
- 4 people holding snowballs

Sleighing in New York (detail), Thomas Benecke, artist; Nagel and Lewis, printer; Emil Seitz, publisher

People from every social class crowd the street in Thomas Benecke's lively winter scene. Snowballs fly through the air and a band plays while a police officer cracks a whip at two sleighs that are about to collide in front of Barnum's Museum. The museum, which attracted as many as 400,000 visitors a year, stood at the corner of Broadway and Ann Street in New York City from 1841 to 1865, when it was destroyed by a fire.

20½ x 30½ in.
The Edward W. C. Arnold Collection of New York Prints, Maps, and Pictures, Bequest of Edward W. C. Arnold, 1954   54.90.1061